Monkey High!
2
I0631106
Fremont Public Library
1170 N. Midlothian Rd.
Mundelein, IL 60060
Story & Art by Shouko Akira

Monkey High!

2

CONTENTS

4th Monkey:
A First Date Is Less Scary Than a Haunted House
3

5th Monkey:
The Most Important Question Can't Be Answered in a Quiz
43

Monkey High! Special Edition
144

Postscript
184

Story Thus Far

Masaru Yamashita
(Nickname: Macharu)

Haruna was forced to transfer to a new school because of her father's involvement in a corruption scandal. She compares her crazy new classmates to a troop of monkeys but finds herself drawn to one of them—Macharu. They establish that they are both attracted to each other and decide to start dating, but...?!

Haruna Aizawa

A FIRST DATE IS LESS SCARY THAN A HAUNTED HOUSE

IT'S NOT AN UNCOMMON STORY...

A SCHOOL BEING LIKE A MOUNTAIN FULL OF MONKEYS...

IT HAPPENS ALL THE TIME.

A PERSON MEETING ANOTHER PERSON AND FALLING IN LOVE...

NONETHELESS, IT'S STILL SURPRISING...

DreamLand
1-DAY PASSPORT
COUPLE TICKETS (LIMITED TIME ONLY)
12.20.200X TO 12.30.200X

Monkey High!

PUSH
GLANCE
WELCOME!
Welcome!
HEY THERE.
HELLO.
WHAT'RE YOU DOING HERE, MASARU?
IT HASN'T EVEN BEEN A MONTH SINCE YOU LAST CAME.

PAT
ATSU!
I didn't think you'd be here.
REALLY?
YOU HAVE A GIRL-FRIEND NOW, MASARU?
YEP. OUR BABY MONKEY HAS A REAL BEAUTY!
HE'S GOT HIS FIRST DATE TOMORROW, MOM!
WHAT?
WHO DO YOU THINK TOLD YOU ABOUT THE DISCOUNTED COUPLE TICKETS AT DREAMLAND?
How quickly we forget.
I OWE YOU NOTHING, MAN.
NOW PLEASE, SIR. WON'T YOU SIT OVER HERE?
WE'LL GIVE YOU A GREAT STYLE!
WHO ASKED YOU?!

YOU KNOW I'M YOUR BIGGEST SUPPORTER!
WANT ME TO GIVE YOU A BUZZ CUT LIKE IN JUNIOR HIGH?!
YOU GUYS DO REALIZE I HAVE CUSTOMERS HERE...
Knock it off, you unlicensed jerk!!
HIS CHRISTMAS PRESENT TO ME...
...WAS THIS FREE PASS.
I HAVEN'T BEEN TO ONE OF THESE PLACES SINCE GRADE SCHOOL...
AN AMUSEMENT PARK?
HE DEFINITELY GAVE THIS TO ME BECAUSE HE WANTS TO GO...

THIS IS OUR FIRST REAL DATE TOGETHER...
IT'S ALSO THE FIRST TIME I'VE SEEN HIM SINCE OUR FIRST KISS...
MAYBE I FEEL A LITTLE EMBARRASSED...
...BECAUSE IT ALL HASN'T SUNK IN YET...
HEY!
HARUNA!
Mornin'!
OVER HERE! I ALREADY GOT OUR TICKETS!
Good morning.
I CAN'T BELIEVE I'M GOING OUT WITH A BABY MONKEY!!
Here ya go!

THANKS.
SORRY. DID YOU WAIT LONG?
WOW! THIS REALLY IS A DATE!
WHAT ARE YOU TALKING ABOUT ?!
SKY HURRICANE
CHECK OUT THAT ROLLER COASTER! IT'S SO AWESOME!!
HEY! I SAW THAT ONE ON TV!
OOH! THEY'VE GOT GO-CARTS TOO!
C'MON, HARUNA! HURRY!
WOULD YOU CALM DOWN!

AAAGHHH!!!

DROP

AHHH!

SHUUU

OH MY GOD!

THE STAFF HERE MUST BE PLEASED TO GET THIS KIND OF REACTION...

EXIT
NICE! I FOUND THE EXIT!
GOOD THING, HUH, HARUNA ?
FOR YOU, MAYBE ...
BRUSH
AHHHH!!
IT'S JUST SOMEONE IN AN ANIMAL SUIT...
...
PUNCH
JEEZ! YOU SCARED ME THERE!
Hey bud.
PUNCH
HEY!
KNOCK
PUNCH
WHAT THE HECK?
You want a piece o' me?
STOP COMPETING WITH EACH OTHER!
You're both monkeys, remember?
MACHARU ...
YOU FIT IN HERE WAY TOO WELL...
Not that I'm surprised...
B'bye!

THAT WOULD HURT MY MANHOOD!
I THINK IT'S TOO LATE TO WORRY ABOUT THAT...
Quit while you're ahead.
YOU DIDN'T HAVE TO GO IF IT'S SOMETHING YOU'RE NOT INTO...
The haunted house, I mean...
ACK. I YELLED TOO MUCH. MY THROAT HURTS.
BUT...
WE CAME HERE TOGETHER.
SO I WANT TO EXPERIENCE THINGS TOGETHER.
EVEN IF I'M LAUGHING AT HOW FREAKED OUT YOU ARE?
URR...
DARN IT!
HA HA HA.

THINGS THAT WE CAN DO TOGETHER...
THINGS THAT FREAK YOU OUT...
YES, EVEN THEN!
AND THINGS THAT MAKE YOU HAPPY...
EVERY-THING...
I WANT TO DO IT ALL.

C'MON.

LET'S GO ON THAT ONE NEXT!
YOU DON'T HAVE TO RUN!
But I want to get on it right away!
Yeah.
That one?
You're hurting my pride, you know...
Hey, there's one called the Mystery House.
Why'd they have to build two haunted houses?!

KNOCK
NOOOOO!
WHAT IS THIS?!
He got ice cream on me!!
This was an expensive coat!
I'll get you a new one.
Sniff...
Sniff...
HOLD IT RIGHT THERE.
SEE THIS CANDY?
NOW WHICH HAND IS IT IN?
...

...THIS ONE?
NICE! YOU WIN!!
HA HA HA
HERE'S THE GRAND PRIZE-THE CANDY PLUS AN EXTRA COIN TOO!
NOW YOU CAN GET A NEW ICE CREAM!
HA HA HA
REALLY? Seems like you'd've loved this sort of thing.
I...
...ACTUALLY CAME A LOT.
MY FAMILY RUNS A STORE, SO MY PARENTS WERE ALWAYS REALLY BUSY.
NOT THAT I REALLY LIKED IT...
HEY! JUST WHAT ARE YOU GETTING AT?
GRR...
OH. That's right.
NOW THAT I THINK ABOUT IT...
...I NEVER CAME TO PLACES LIKE THIS AS A KID.

I REMEMBER...
...MY FATHER BRINGING ME SOMETIMES...
BACK WHEN I STILL LIKED HIM...
Hm...
SO YOU DON'T REALLY HAVE ANY CHILDHOOD MEMORIES OF GOING TO THE AMUSEMENT PARK?
NOPE. BUT WHEN I WAS IN FOURTH GRADE...
...ATSU SAID, "I'LL TAKE YA!"
SO WE SNUCK OUT.

Hey!
Macharu!
Atsu!
AND? WHAT HAPPENED?
I WAVED AT ATSU FROM DOWN BELOW.
AH HA HA HA!
That's so like him to get on it without you!
BUT I WASN'T TALL ENOUGH AND...
120 cm
You Must Be Taller Than Me
HA HA HA.
BUT WE PRETTY MUCH USED ALL THE MONEY WE HAD JUST GETTING THERE.
WE DECIDED TO JUST GET ON THE ROLLER COASTER SINCE THAT'S WHAT WE CAME FOR.
WE USED THE REST OF THE MONEY TO GO ON THE TEACUP RIDE...
Teacups
Adult: $4
Child: $2
We could both get on this one.
You're right!
Fool
NOW THAT I THINK ABOUT IT... HEY, ATSU GOT TO GO ON TWO RIDES!!
The roller coaster AND the teacups!!
AH HA HA HA HA!
Stop it! You're killing me!

MOMMY! WILL YOU BUY ME A BALLOON ?!
RUMBLE
AHHHH!
Would the mother of...
BUSTLE
BUSTLE
HA HA HA!
Wait!
WHAT THE HECK ARE WE DOING?!
IN PLAIN VIEW...!
UNBELIEVABLE !!
WHAT SHOULD WE GET ON NEXT?
UH...
UM...
MAP

WELL...
LET'S TRY THE ROLLER COASTER...
CHUK
CHUK
CHUK
CHUK
CHUK
CHUK
HARUNA... THIS ONE TWISTS AND FALLS A LOT...
IS THAT OKAY?
YEAH.
YOU LIKE THESE, RIGHT?
YUP. LOVE 'EM.

WHA...
DROP
GROAOO
WOOOOH!
KYAAAA!!

CHUNK
HARUNA ?
YOU OKAY...?
ACK!
HARUNA !!
MY HEAD'S SPINNING ...
HANG ON! I'LL GET YOU SOMETHING TO DRINK!
THIS... SUCKS ...
HEEEEEY.
WHAT'S WRONG? ARE YOU LOST?

Dude, she's super hot.
DOESN'T LOOK LIKE YOU'RE FEELING TOO GOOD.
WE DROVE HERE. WANT A LIFT HOME?
SERIOUSLY? THEY'RE PICKING UP GIRLS AT AN AMUSEMENT PARK?!
STUMPED
WE SORT OF LOST THE PEOPLE WE WERE WITH...
...SO WE WERE THINKING OF TAKING OFF ANYWAY.
NO THANKS ...
I'M HERE WITH SOME-BODY...
HARUNA.
WHAT? A GUY? A GIRL?
IF YOU'RE HERE WITH GIRLS, THEN...
I BROUGHT YOU SOME TEA.
YOUR LITTLE BROTHER?
...

CAN YOU GET UP, HARUNA?
LET'S GO OVER THERE.
NOW, NOW. YOUR SISTER LOOKS LIKE SHE'S IN PAIN.
LET US TAKE CARE OF HER.
ALL RIGHT, NOW COME OVER HERE.
KICK
GET YOUR HANDS OFF OF HER.
YOU LITTLE...
DO YOU KNOW WHAT YOU JUST DID, YOU SHRIMP?!

SMACK
MACHARU!
PUNCH
SOME-ONE...
SOME-ONE WHO WORKS HERE ...
Ha!
YOU LITTLE PUNK!

SMACK
WHOA!
A...
...MONKEY?!
KNOCK
PUNCH
AH!
OWW!
HEY...
WHAT'S GOING ON?
A monkey!
IS THIS SOME KIND OF SHOW?

Is this a performance?
Wow! Look at the monkey!
GATHER GATHER
...
It's over already?
No fun.
This is too weird...
Umm... EXCUSE ME...
Hey! You guys okay?!

HEY NOW! NO VIOLENCE AT AMUSEMENT PARKS!
This is the land of dreams, man.
That was crazy.
WASN'T EVEN THAT GREAT AS AN ATTRACTION EITHER.
EHR NOT GIVEN
WHA...
WHAT'RE YOU GUYS DOING HERE?!
WE'RE OBVIOUSLY HERE TO HAVE A GOOD TIME.
Duh.
IT'S WINTER BREAK.
PLUS ATSU GAVE US DISCOUNT TICKETS!
POP
HUH?
Atsu did?

AGH, IT'S HOT IN HERE...
THIS IS LIKE THE BEST DIET EVER.
ATSU!
YO.
WHA...
WHAT'RE YOU...!
I'M GETTING PAID TO DO THIS, OBVIOUSLY.
NOTHIN' BETTER TO DO SINCE SOMEONE I KNOW HAS A GIRLFRIEND NOW.
I WAS TALKING TO THESE GUYS OVER THERE...
I SAW HARUNA GETTING MESSED WITH, SO...
BUT ANYWAY. HAVE YOU GUYS BEEN ON THE FERRIS WHEEL?
YOU CAN'T MISS IT THIS TIME OF THE DAY, MAN.
Go make out while you watch the sunset.

DROP
HARUNA ?!
YOU OKAY ?!
TATUM
TATUM
TATUM
TATUM
TATUM
TATUM
TATUM
TATUM
TATUM
TATUM
YOU SURE YOU'RE ALL RIGHT?
YEAH...
I guess I was just exhausted...
I'M SORRY WE COULDN'T STAY TILL THE END...
DON'T WORRY ABOUT IT.

I'M SORRY.
GEEZ...
WHY DID THIS HAPPEN TO ME...?
This sucks.
IT WAS TOO MUCH FROM THE BEGINNING...
I WAS SO EXCITED I DIDN'T THINK ABOUT WHAT YOU WANTED...
NOT TO MENTION WHAT HAPPENED AT THE END...
I'M SORRY.
NISHIMACHI! NEXT STOP, NISHIMACHI!
THAT'S...

THAT'S NOT TRUE...
LET'S GET OFF.
I WAS TOO...
YOU WEREN'T THE ONLY ONE EXCITED...
THIS IS FINE. THANKS.

BUT I WAS SO HAPPY.
SORRY FOR BEING SO HYPER.
HARUNA...
I KNOW YOU MAY NOT LIKE...
...AMUSEMENT PARKS AND THAT KIND OF THING, SO...
THANKS!

SEE
I'll giv
you a ri

MACHARU!

I LIKE YOU...

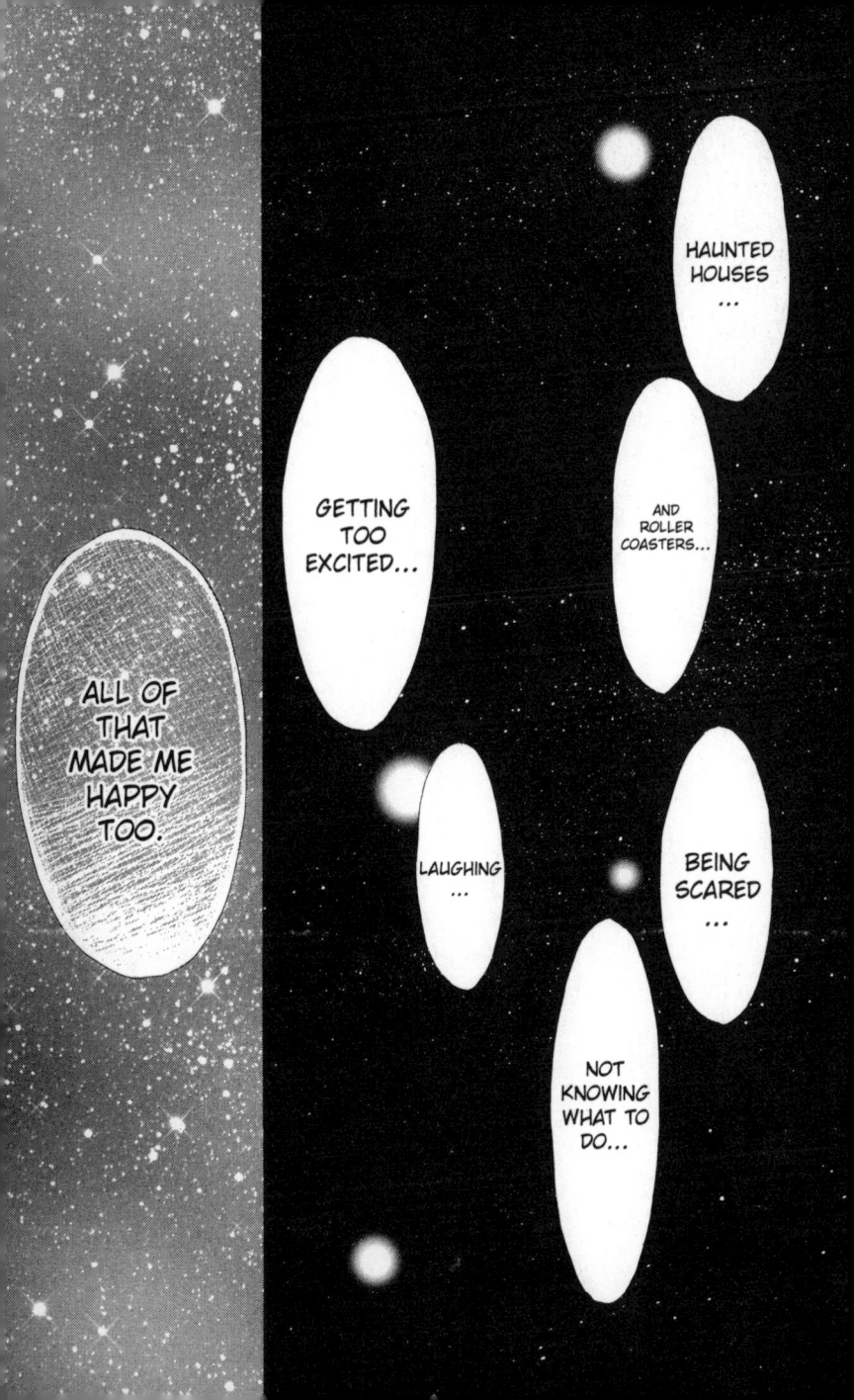
HAUNTED HOUSES ...
GETTING TOO EXCITED...
AND ROLLER COASTERS...
ALL OF THAT MADE ME HAPPY TOO.
LAUGHING ...
BEING SCARED ...
NOT KNOWING WHAT TO DO...

BECAUSE I WAS WITH YOU...
WELL ...
I'LL SEE YOU LATER!
NEXT TIME, LET'S GO ON THE FERRIS WHEEL TOO!
HEY!
HARUNA !

THIS IS STILL...
...LIKE BEING IN WONDERLAND...

HAVING HOPES OR BEING DISAPPOINTED...

BEING HAPPY OR ANGRY...

HAVING FUN TOGETHER OR BEING ANXIOUS...

WONDERING...

...WHAT THE FUTURE HOLDS FOR US...

AND WANTING TO JUST RUN WITH IT.

"WHERE SHOULD WE GO NEXT?"

"ANYWHERE!"

IT'S AS IF THAT'S THE ENTIRE WORLD...

MEMBERS OF THE SAME GROUP CONSTANTLY FIGHT AND GET BACK TOGETHER AGAIN...

SCHOOL LIFE'S LIKE BEING ON A MOUNTAIN FULL OF MONKEYS...

BUT...

FROM THE OUTSIDE, IT'S AN AMAZINGLY SMALL WORLD.

QUESTION CAN'T BE
IN A QUIZ

THE MOST IMPORTANT
ANSWERED

1/7 Commencement 9:30
Homeroom 10:00~
Cleaning 10:30~
THE NEW SEMESTER STARTS TODAY.
THE GUYS IN THE INNER COURT ARE TOTALLY SLACKING OFF!
HEY!
WHERE'S THE DUST-PAN?
Don't throw it over here!
EWWWW! THIS RAG REEKS!
HARUNA AIZAWA
15 YEARS OLD
FIRST YEAR IN HIGH SCHOOL
THEY SAID THEY'VE GOT LUNCH ON THE LINE!
What?! Oh, that's just so typical!
CAN THESE PEOPLE EVER STAY QUIET...?

Go, Atsu!
SO YOU THINK YOU CAN STOP ME, HUH?
BMP
AND YOU THINK YOU CAN GET BY ME, HUH?
Bring it on!
YEAH---
WE'RE ROOTIN' FOR YA, ATSU!
THANKS, GIRLS!
FOCUS, MAN!!

Ha ha ha.
HEY, HARUNA. COME OVER AND CHECK IT OUT.
NOT REALLY THAT ENTERTAINING, IS IT?
WHAT'RE YOU TALKING ABOUT?
GO ROOT FOR YOUR BOYFRIEND!
C'mon!
TUG
WA...
MACHARUUU!
HARUNA'S WATCHING YOU!!

SMILE
C'MON, ATSU! SHOW ME WHAT YOU'VE GOT!
IT'S BEEN FOUR MONTHS SINCE I TRANS-FERRED HERE...
Like I'm gonna lose to someone like you!
Dude, now you're just being mean...

CONFESSION
I'VE TEASED MYSELF ABOUT IT A HUNDRED TIMES...
APPROACH
CONTACT
I DON'T KNOW HOW THIS...
...ALL HAPPENED EXACTLY...
Yeah!
THIS CLASS IS LIKE A TROOP OF MONKEYS, AND...
THIS IS THE BABY→ MONKEY.
MASARU YAMASHITA (NICKNAMED MACHARU)
SHOVE
GO, MACHARU! SHOOT THE BALL!
CAN YA DO IT?!
YEAH!
AND HE IS MY BOY-FRIEND...

HEY.
OH...
BOOM
KNOCK
BANG
CRASH
ALMOST EVERY DAY...
...SOMETHING UNBELIEVABLE HAPPENS...
PRINCIPAL'S OFFICE

YOU!!
AREN'T YOU ASHAMED OF YOURSELVES? YOU'RE IN HIGH SCHOOL, FOR CRYING OUT LOUD!
I'M SORRY...
Sorry.
Great. The other jerks just went home...
IT JUST HAD TO GO INTO THE PRINCIPAL'S OFFICE, DIDN'T IT...
WELL, MR. FURUKAWA...
IT SEEMS THAT THEY FEEL BADLY ABOUT IT.
BUT...
IT'S LIKE THEY SAY... "NOTHING LASTS FOREVER..."
Ha ha.
HE'S DEFINITELY CRYING...
THAT VASE WAS REALLY SPECIAL TO HIM...
I always saw him polishing it and looking at it.

HMM...
WELL, I GUESS WE HAVE TO PAY HIM BACK THEN...
We'll split it between all of us.
IT WAS IMARI PORCELAIN, WASN'T IT?
I'M SURE IT COSTS ABOUT TEN THOUSAND DOLLARS...
FRE
EZE
IT'S HOPELESS. WHERE WOULD WE GET THAT KIND OF MONEY?
WE COULD ALL GET JOBS.
WITH SIX PEOPLE... HOW MUCH WOULD EACH OF US HAVE TO MAKE?
HEY, LEAVE US OUT OF IT!
Why're you including us in the headcount?
HMM.
WAIT A SEC.
TEN THOUSAND DOLLARS...
I READ SOME-THING ABOUT IT IN A MAGAZINE TODAY...
FLIP FLIP
TV Guide

THERE IT IS!!
TV Sponsored
QUIZ SHOW CHAMPIONSHIP
HIGH SCHOOL EDITION
PRIZE: a whopping $10,000!!
☆Teams of six: all members must
☆Must be able to make it to locat
...I'M NOT DOING THAT.
Oh my God! Look who the celebrity guest is!!
IT'S A SIGN!!
PLUS, IT'S A TEAM OF SIX!
OH, I'VE SEEN THAT SHOW.
WOW!!
Ten thousand dollars!!
HARUNA!
C'MON, MACHARU! YOU'VE GOT TO CONVINCE YOUR GIRL!
BUT YOU'RE THE SMARTEST.
I THINK IT'S OBVIOUS...
HUH?! WHY NOT?!

Please?
YOU'VE GOT TO DO THIS FOR THE PRINCIPAL!
I'M SORRY, BUT I'M NOT THAT ATTACHED TO THE PRINCIPAL...
...
BUT HE'S SO NICE!!
He makes us snacks and stuff.
BUT YOU GUYS ARE THE ONES WHO BROKE HIS VASE...
THEN, HARUNA ...
YOU SHOULD DO IT FOR MACHARU!
Exactly!
ANY PET'S MISTAKE IS THE RESPONSIBILITY OF ITS OWNER!!
WHAT ?!
I ALREADY ENTERED US.
Via cell phone.
HUH?! WAIT A SEC!

I DON'T BELIEVE THIS...
A QUIZ... A QUIZ SHOW...
Who goes on those things? I mean, who breaks vases?!
BUT IT SOUNDS KINDA FUN...
WELL, MAYBE FOR YOU...
YEAH, BUT...
I HAVE MORE FUN DOING THINGS WHEN YOU'RE AROUND.
SURE...
IT'S TRUE.
We've gotta train starting tomorrow!
WHY...
...IS IT YOU...
...I WONDER?

AND I WONDER... WHY ME?
Train? For a quiz show?
OKAY.
I'LL SEE YOU TOMORROW.
THANKS.
NO PROB.

OKAY!
B'BYE!
SQUEAK
DOES HE NOT CARE ABOUT OTHER PEOPLE SEEING...?
Dork.
WHY...

603
AIZAWA
So unbelievable...
OPEN
I STILL CAN'T BELIEVE I'M WITH MACHARU.
...DO I SECOND-GUESS EVERYTHING...
I'M HOME...
...LIKE A CHILD?
YES?
SHUT
I GOT A PHONE CALL TODAY...
HARUNA ...

HE'S DONE SERVING HIS TIME. HE'S COMING HOME.
YOUR FATHER...
SO?
FWEE
FWEE
HARUNA ...
IF YOU WANT TO SEE HIM, YOU CAN GO TO THE OFFICE...
IT DOESN'T MATTER.
KREE
WHO KNOWS ...
I'M SURE HE'LL BE VERY BUSY.
Ha.
NOTHING SEEMS TO CHANGE.
HERE?
HE'S COMING ?

SIX MONTHS AGO...
SLAM
I'M BUSY TOO.
DIET MEMBER SHINICHI AIZAWA ARRESTED ON BRIBERY CHARGES
...AND WE WERE FORCED TO LEAVE THE HOUSE AND THE TOWN THAT WE LIVED IN.
MY POLITICIAN FATHER GOT ARRESTED FOR BEING INVOLVED IN A CORRUPTION SCANDAL...
IT'S...
...MY FAMILY WAS ...
...BROKEN LONG BEFORE THEN...
BUT I THINK ...
...TOO LATE.

QUESTION...
SWIFT
"BANANAS ARE SNACKS!"
True or false?!
Oh, come on!
WHAT KIND OF QUESTION IS THAT?!
WE'VE GOT TWO TRUES AND TWO FALSES.
YOU'VE GOT THE DECIDING VOTE, HARUNA.
SINCE WHEN DID IT BECOME A MAJORITY VOTE?!
WE CAN'T HAVE MACHARU ASK THE QUESTIONS...
Yeah.
THEY'RE ALL ABOUT FOOD.
THESE PEOPLE ARE MORONS...
Although I am nailing them all
Yep.

But my parents own a produce store.
That's no excuse.
ARE YOU BORED?
YOU'VE BEEN SIGHING ALL DAY.
I'M JUST AMAZED ...
HARUNA ...
IT'S JUST SO STUPID...

I THINK WE SHOULD TRY TO COVER CURRENT AFFAIRS.
WANNA GO TO THE LIBRARY ?
YOU'RE MISSING THE POINT!
SO YOU WOULD'VE RATHER DONE THE COSTUME CONTEST?
IT'S THE POWER OF LOVE!
THAT'S NOT WHAT...
NICE! SHE'S FINALLY ON BOARD!!
Yes!
"HE'S COMING HOME."
It's a probability thing.
It's just luck, man.
You've gotta go with your gut instinct for the True and False part.
Shut up.
Coach!
Let's call her "Coach" from now on.

I HAVE MY OWN LIFE TO LIVE...
ALBEIT PARTICIPATING IN A QUIZ SHOW...
Quiz Strategies
BOOM
BOOM
POP POP POP
TV SPONSORED QUIZ SHOW CHAMPIONSHIP HIGH SCHOOL EDITION QUALIFICATION
MINAMIGAOKA PARK
IT DOESN'T MATTER ...

Francisko (Girl in spirit)
Xavier (Male)
HELLO, EVERY-BODY! ♡
WE'RE THE COMIC DUO FRANCISKO XAVIER!
ARE YOU ALL EXCITED?!
YEAH--
No way.
I CAN'T BELIEVE HOW CROWDED IT IS...
IT SEEMS THE WORLD IS FULL OF IDIOTS AND SLACKERS.
AND YOU'RE ONE OF THEM!
Please. I'm trying not to see it that way...
ONLY SIX TEAMS CAN MAKE IT TO THE FINAL ROUND A WEEK FROM TODAY!
SO THE BEST OF LUCK TO YOU ALL!
LET'S GET STARTED ON THE FIRST ROUND!
THE RUNNING YOUTH HILL!

WHAT IS THIS?
A hike?
HEY! WE'RE WEARING BOOTS!
NOW YOU ALL START TOGETHER ON QUESTION 1!
"THERE IS SUCH A THING AS TWIN MONKEYS." TRUE OR FALSE?!
First stage
FINISH
Question 6
YOU HAVE TO RUN UP THE HILL AND ANSWER THE QUESTIONS.
GET THE ANSWER RIGHT AND YOU CONTINUE UP. BUT ANSWER INCORRECTLY AND YOU MOVE BACK DOWN.
Question 2
MAKE IT TO THE TOP TO AVOID BEING ELIMINATED!
Question 1

YEAH
Ouw! I tripped!
STOMP
STOMP
STOMP
Hey! Don't push me!
WHICH IS IT, MACHARU?!
UMMM ...
I MEAN, WHY'RE YOU ASKING ME?!
YOU SHOULD KNOW!
What?
FALSE ...
I MEAN ...
TRUE!
THE ANSWER IS TRUE!
NICE
I knew it!
ONLY THE TEAMS THAT ANSWERED CORRECTLY MAY PROCEED TO THE NEXT GATE.
WOW...
HARUNA.
IT'S A TROOP OF MONKEYS, ALL RIGHT...
A really big one at that.

QUESTION TWO

TRANSLATE THE FOLLOWING PHRASE INTO ENGLISH:

「終わりよければすべてよし」

A

SCRIBBLE SCRIBBLE
SHUP
WE'RE ALLOWED TO LOOK AT DICTIONARIES, RIGHT?
HEY!
English Dictionary
UMM...
End...?
All's well that ends well.
CORRECT!!
ARRGHH!!
WHOO-HOO!
YEAH, HARUNA !!
DUDE, THIS IS EASY!
EASY FOR YOU TO SAY.

CONGRATULATIONS! YOU'VE CLEARED THE FIRST ROUND!
YAAAY!
BAVARIAN CREAM.
Loving food really paid off... Huh, Kobu!
Kobuhei Kohei Matsumoto
BAVARIAN CREAM, PUDDING, AND JELLO-WHICH ONE GOT ITS NAME FROM AN ACTUAL PLACE?
LIBERO!
Class officer Yuko Kawano Good at sports.
WHAT ITALIAN WORD FOR "FREE MAN" IS A POSITION BOTH IN SOCCER AND IN VOLLEYBALL?
EROS! EROS!
You looked that up in the dictionary before, didn't you?!
Loves chicks ♡ Atsuyuki Kido
IN ROMAN MYTHOLOGY, IT WAS CUPID. WHO IS KNOWN AS THE GOD OF LOVE IN GREEK MYTHOLOGY?
I've got this one!
FOURTEEN!
Emi Tejima I've got my celebrities down!
ADD THE MEMBERS OF ARASHI, W-INDS, AND KAT-TUN AND HOW MANY PEOPLE DO YOU HAVE?

HI, EVERYONE. ARE YOU GUYS ALL IN THE SAME CLASS?
Ooh. What a cute boy.
WE'RE GOING TO INTERVIEW THE TEAMS THAT ARE LEFT!
OKAY NOW!
WE'RE CLASS 1-2 AT KITAYAMA HIGH SCHOOL.
PLEASE SEND FAN LETTERS TO ATSUYUKI KIDO AT THE ADDRESS BELOW!
DO YOU MIND ADDING MY ADDRESS THERE LATER?
His self PR is amazing.
SO THIS IS A COED TEAM!
ARE THERE ANY COUPLES IN THE GROUP?
I'd love to know.
YEP!
THESE TWO ARE INSEPARABLE!
I wouldn't have thought...
YOU'VE GOT IT WRONG!
We're not...?
This idiot...
YOU CAN BE INSEPARABLE FROM ME.

I'm hungry.
I wonder if they'll feed us lunch.
Ha.
YOU'RE RIGHT. BESIDES, I BELONG TO EVERYBODY.
ATSU! YOU CAN'T BREAK UP THE HAPPY COUPLE.
It was just a joke...
I JUST DON'T WANT TO LOSE TO THAT TEAM...
Cute!
Wanna go talk to him later?
His name's Atsuyuki!
M High School Quiz Club
ER... WHAT A LIVELY BUNCH!
WE WON THE SECOND AND THIRD ROUND...
AFTER THAT...
...WE WERE UNSTOPPABLE. WE CLEARED EVERY DIFFICULT QUESTION THROWN OUR WAY.

THE $10K IS OURS! DEAR PRINCIPAL--WE'LL GET YOUR VASE SOON!!
...AND EVEN WON A PLACE IN THE FINAL SHOW!
I'M IMPRESSED! WE WERE SO LUCKY!
THERE WERE SO MANY QUESTIONS WE KNEW.
IT WAS PROBABLY THE PRINCIPAL LOOKING OUT FOR US.
DON'T TALK ABOUT HIM LIKE HE'S DEAD.
HEY!
YOU GUYS! WAIT!
WHAT?
HEY, YOU...
I KNEW IT!

YOU'RE THE DIET MEMBER SHINICHI AIZAWA'S DAUGHTER, RIGHT?
UMM... HARUNA AIZAWA...
YOU USED TO GO TO K ACADEMY, RIGHT?
WHO THE HECK ARE YOU?
WE'RE FROM O TV...
...AND WE'D LOVE TO HEAR YOUR STORY.
MR. AIZAWA WAS RELEASED THE OTHER DAY, RIGHT?
HOW'S HE DOING? HAVE YOU TALKED TO HIM?
RUMOR HAS IT THAT HE'S SEPARATED FROM HIS WIFE.

SMAK
IS IT BECAUSE OF THE INCIDENT ...?
WE'RE NOT OBLIGATED TO ANSWER ANY QUESTION OUTSIDE OF THE GAME SHOW.

WAI...
JUST ...
...A FEW MORE QUES...
LET'S GO, HARUNA.
DON'T YOU KNOW YOU'RE BEING RUDE, MAN?
HEY!
KICK
WE'LL SUE YOU FOR HA-RASSMENT, MISTER.

IT'S OKAY.
WE CAN...
...STOP NOW.
MA... MACHARU...
TUG TUG TUG
YOU OKAY?
YEAH ...
I GOT THAT A LOT BEFORE.
JUST SIX MONTHS AGO...
...THEY WERE ALL OVER MY HOUSE AND SCHOOL.
SO I'M USED TO IT...
THAT'S NOT WHAT I'M ASKING.

YOU'RE KINDA...
GRAB
Whoa!
YOU DON'T NEED TO LOOK SO SERIOUS.
WELL ...
knot
OKAY.

THANKS.
You look like a kid from up north.
What's that supposed to mean?
RING RING
Ah ha ha.
NOW YOU LOOK EVEN YOUNGER.

LET'S GO ON A DATE!
IT'S FROM EMI.
WE R GONNA GO HOME. HV FUN U 2. THERES A FERRIS WHEEL CLOSE BY U KNOW.
...WHAT DO YOU WANT TO DO?

NOW THAT I THINK ABOUT IT...
HARUNA'S DAD'S A POLITICIAN, HUH?
I TOTALLY FORGOT.
HMM ...
IT WAS ALL OVER THE NEWS WHEN IT FIRST HAPPENED.
The paparazzi went nuts.
Y'KNOW, WHEN HARUNA FIRST TRANSFERRED, SHE WAS SO JADED.
YEP.
BUT NOW SHE'S A MONKEY KEEPER.
Yep
I wonder why Macharu? She's so hot.
THAT'S THE BEAUTY OF LOVE.
Though honestly, I don't get it either.
It's what they call puppy love. Or maybe she's just an animal lover?
I think she's been put under some-kinda dark spell.
She'll come to her senses soon.

WOW! CHECK IT OUT!!
WHAT'S THAT? IT'S ALL LIT UP!
COME LOOK, HARUNA!
MACHARU...
YOU'RE MAKING IT SHAKE... SIT.
OOPS.
SHMP
SORRY.

PLOP
IT'S...
IT'S KIND OF CROWDED, ISN'T IT?
A bit...
YEAH.
BUT...
...IT'S PRETTY ROOMY TOO.

OH...
IT'S SNOWING!
AW, NO! I HAVE TO HELP WITH THE INSPECTION AT THE STORE!
INSPECTION? OF THE PRODUCE STORE?
YEAH. WE'VE GOT TO CHECK THE PRODUCE AND CLEAN UP...
BUT IT'S SO COLD!!
And you can't use heaters...
HA HA HA.
Really?
Even with two pairs of socks on!
THEN YOU SHOULD GET HOME SOON.
YEAH ...
BUT ...
I'LL TAKE YOU HOME FIRST.
IT'S ALREADY DARK.
I'LL BE FINE. I'M NEAR HERE.
Pretty close by.
BUT...
PLUS, WON'T YOUR MOM THROW A FIT IF YOU GET HOME LATE?
YOU'RE LATE!
SMACK
SEEN IT HAPPEN ONCE
URRR...

YOU'RE RIGHT. SHE WOULD DO THAT...
HA HA HA.
BYE!
SO...
I'M FINE HERE.
OH.
OKAY.
It's coming down now.
HUFF
BUT...
IT'S PROBABLY PRETTY COLD AT THE PRODUCE STORE...
MACHARU'S HOUSE PROBABLY FEELS...
...PRETTY WARM.

SEE YOU LATER, ATSU! ♡
YEAH! SEE YOU LATER.
Brr. It's cold.
BUM BA DUM
HEY, HARUNA!
WHERE'S MACHARU?
Did he go home?
PAT

SHA
OH...

HEY!
WAI...
HEY!
WHAT THE HECK HAPPENED ...?
DID MACHARU ...?

"WHAT'S THE MOST IMPORTANT THING YOU LOOK AT WHEN YOU'RE LOOKING AT A WOMAN?"
Um...
HER SKIRT?
EEEEH!
HER LEGS, OBVIOUSLY!
And her butt.
What's that?!
HEY, ATSU. IT'S YOUR TURN TO PEDAL, MAN.
HMM...
THEN, ONE LAST QUESTION.
DID SOMETHING HAPPEN WITH HARUNA YESTERDAY?
WHA... WHAT DO YOU MEAN BY THAT?
I MEAN, AFTER YOU SPLIT FROM THE REST OF US.
AFTER THAT...
WE GOT ON THE FERRIS WHEEL AND...
AND...

POOF
HEY!
WHAT IS IT?!
DID YOU ...?
KNOCK IT OFF!
You're gonna make me crash!
SPIT IT OUT!
WHAT'D YOU DO?!
YOU PUSHED HER DOWN? FELT HER UP?
WHAT ?!
THAT'S NO GOOD, MAN.
I KNOW THE FERRIS WHEEL PUTS YOU IN THE MOOD, BUT OF COURSE THAT KIND OF STUFF'LL PUSH HER TO TEARS!
I DIDN'T DO ANY-THING!
SCREECH
WHAT DID YOU SAY?
HUH?
TEARS...?
WHO...?

HARUNA WAS...
WHEN I SAW HER LAST NIGHT...

...WHY?
WAS SHE CRYING IN FRONT OF YOU?

I DUNNO.
LOOKS LIKE...
...YOU'RE THE ONE WHO HAS TO SOLVE IT.
I'm stopping off at the convenience store.
I GUESS THAT'S THE BIGGER MYSTERY THEN.
HE PROBABLY TOTALLY MISUNDER-STOOD THAT.
OH WELL.
He was getting on my nerves.

SO DID YOU GO HOME AND HELP OUT?
Your family, I mean?
OH.
YEAH.
GOOD MORNING.

THEY MADE ME SCRUB RADISHES UNTIL ONE IN THE MORNING.
HA HA HA.

WHERE'S ATSU?
Didn't you come here together?
HE SAID HE HAD TO STOP OFF SOME-WHERE...
OH.
PHEW
DONG DONG DONG DONG DONG
Oh...
LET'S GO SIT DOWN.
I KNOW I'M GOING TO GET CALLED ON TODAY.

THEY'RE FILMING IT NEXT SUNDAY, SO COME CHEER US ON!
SO YOU'RE GONNA BE ON TV?
YEAH. IT WAS A BREEZE.
WHAT?? YOU GUYS GOT THROUGH THE PRELIMINARY ROUND?!
MAYBE WE'LL GO AND MAKE POSTERS FOR EACH OF YOU.
MAYBE EVEN ADD SOME CATCH-PHRASES?
Like "The Last Samurai" or "The Japanese Headquarters."
THEN I WANNA BE "THE SMILING PRINCE"!
YOU MEAN LIKE IN THAT KOREAN TV DRAMA? That's not hip anymore.
WHAT ABOUT FOR MACHARU?
"I CAME FROM NIKKO."
Or "The Talking Monkey."
THAT SUCKS!
I'M GLAD ATSU HASN'T SAID ANYTHING TO ME.
HARUNA CAN BE "THE MONKEY KEEPER" OR "PET GIRL."
PLEASE, NO.
No on the poster thing altogether.
You just called me fat.
Kobu can be "This is what the world calls fat."

ALL RIGHT! WE'RE REALLY GONNA GET SERIOUS ABOUT TRAINING NOW!!
RING RING
Training?
HELLO ?
MOM?
I'M STILL AT SCHOOL...
What?
HUH?
THE HOSPI-TAL?
ALL RIGHT.
I'LL TALK TO YOU LATER.
... OKAY.
I UNDER-STAND.
IS EVERYTHING OKAY?
SHUT

I GUESS HE COLLAPSED FROM FATIGUE.
IT'S MY FATHER.
DIDN'T YOU JUST SAY "HOSPITAL" ...?
...NOT REALLY.
I'M SORRY! I WAS EAVESDROPPING!
MY MOM WAS JUST CALLING TO SAY SHE'S GOING TO THE HOSPITAL.
BUT IT'S NOT THAT BIG OF A DEAL.
WHAT?!
YOU SHOULD GO TOO.
I'LL GIVE YOU A LIFT ON MY BIKE.
YOU MUST BE WORRIED.
BUT...
HE'LL BE FINE.
You're over-reacting

LET'S GO.
HUH?
WAI...
I SAID IT'S FINE!!
SNAP
DON'T YOU REMEMBER WHAT THE TV GUYS SAID?
MY FATHER WAS NEVER AT HOME ANYWAY.

SO IT DOESN'T MATTER.
IF...
YOU WOULDN'T UNDER-STAND...
IF THAT'S THE CASE...
...THEN IT'S ALL THE MORE REASON TO...
...MACHARU.
THIS DOESN'T CONCERN YOU.

SO LEAVE ME ALONE.

VROOM
HEY...
SHUT UP.
HARUNA WENT HOME.
WHAT... DID YOU GUYS FIGHT?
YOU DID SOME-THING TO MAKE HER MAD, DIDN'T YOU?
Huh?
The monkey's pouting.
What a little punk.
"YOU WOULDN'T UNDERSTAND, MACHARU."
PSUU
NEXT STOP-- SAKANOUE.
SAKANOUE.

I DIDN'T MEAN TO...
...BE SO MEAN...
IT WAS CONVENIENT TO NOT BE ABLE TO THINK WHEN I DIDN'T WANT TO...
...CAME DOWN WITH A FEVER AS IF I WILLED IT.
AFTER THAT ...
...I...

SHE WON'T ANSWER HER CELL, SO YOU'VE GOTTA GO SEE HER.
... YEAH ... BUT...
FOR GOD'S SAKE! JUST GO MAKE UP, WILL YOU!
RUB RUB
AGHHH!
IT'S BEEN FOUR DAYS NOW.
YOU KNOW ...
WHEN I WALK HARUNA HOME, SHE ALWAYS SAYS "THIS IS FINE" WAY BEFORE WE GET TO HER PLACE.

DON'T BE AN IDIOT. TO GET YOURSELF IN THE DOOR, IT'S ALL ABOUT TECHNIQUE.
That's the problem with you amateurs.
IT'S PROBABLY THAT...
...SHE DOESN'T WANT PEOPLE COMING OVER.
ESPECIALLY WITH WHAT'S GOING ON WITH HER FAMILY.
IT'S JUST...
I FEEL LIKE THERE'S A...
... BARRIER ...
WELL...
I'M SURE THERE'RE THINGS SHE'D RATHER NOT TALK ABOUT EVEN IF YOU TWO ARE GOING OUT.

IT'S NOT LIKE YOU CAN DO ANYTHING ABOUT IT JUST BECAUSE YOU KNOW ABOUT HER PROBLEMS.
jingle-
jingle--
jingle-jingle---
WOOOW----
HERE AT O TV'S SPECIAL STUDIO, WE'LL BE SEEING A YOUNG BATTLE OF THE WITS!
IT'S FINALLY HERE! THE QUIZ CHAMPIONSHIP HIGH SCHOOL EDITION FINAL!

OUR CONTESTANTS WILL BE ENTERING THE STUDIO NOW.
M HIGH SCHOOL QUIZ CLUB TEAM.
NOOOOO!
HARUNA'S STILL NOT HERE!
WE'RE JUST GONNA HAVE TO MAKE DO WITHOUT HER.
HEY! IT'S OUR TURN!
YES
KITAYAMA HIGH SCHOOL CLASS 1-2 TEAM.
I ♥ LOVE My Principal
WOOOW
GOOD LUCK, GUYS!
TAKE THE PRIZE 2-5 KITA-HIGH!
1-2
IT SEEMS THAT YOU ONLY HAVE FIVE MEMBERS ...
ONE'S OUT SICK! BUT WE GOT THE DETERMINATION OF SIX.

THE FINAL'S PROBABLY STARTING NOW...
OH...
I WONDER IF THEY'RE ALL MAD AT ME...
...IT'S NOT LIKE I WAS EVER IN THE MOOD TO BE ON A QUIZ SHOW IN THE FIRST PLACE...
I MEAN...
I'M IN NO MOOD TO BE ON A QUIZ SHOW RIGHT NOW...
BUT...

YEAH! A QUIZ SHOW!!
IT'S JUST THAT THOSE IDIOTS...
IT'S JUST THAT...
IT DOESN'T MATTER IF HE DOESN'T UNDERSTAND.
I'D RATHER IT BE THAT WAY.
"YOU WOULDN'T UNDERSTAND, MACHARU!"

WITH EVERYONE...
"IT'S KIND OF CROWDED, ISN'T IT?"
"YEAH."
"BUT IT'S ROOMY TOO."
WITH ME...
I WANT YOUR LAUGH...
...TO BE CAREFREE.

MOM?
I THOUGHT YOU WENT SHOPPI...
HARUNA?
THAT'S ALL I NEED...
SO...
...WHY...
...DO I HURT HIM ...?
KLAK KLAK
SHUT

"THE WORD FOR THE MIND IN ENGLISH THAT ALSO REFERS TO PEOPLE WITH A HIGH DEGREE OF INTELLECT..."
YES!
BING
DAD...
DING DING
BRAIN.
EH EEEH
BRAIMEN!!
BING

WE WERE COUNTING ON HARUNA TO BE THE BRAINS OF THE TEAM.
Right...
I ♥ LOVE
NOOO! THE POINT DIFFERENCE IS GETTING BIGGER.
Agh! Sorry.
You stupid monkey!
KITAYAMA HIGH SCHOOL GETS POINTS DEDUCTED.
IN ORDER TO ANSWER THE QUESTIONS, YOU HAVE TO REACH THE MAX ON THE GAUGE ATTACHED TO THE TREADMILL!
OUR NEXT ROUND IS THE RUNNING QUIZ!
ME?
YOU GO FIRST, MACHARU!
Run!
THIS'LL REALLY HURT US IF WE GET THE ANSWER WRONG.
Physically, that is...
I ♥ LOVE
My Principal
WE'RE ONE SHORT TOO...
That's gonna be rough.
EWWW. I DON'T WANT TO DO THAT.
IT'S A BATTLE OF THE MIND AND BODY.

That's going to be our strategy!!
IT DOESN'T MATTER IF WE KNOW THE ANSWER OR NOT!
SHUT UP AND RUN WITH EVERYTHING YOU'VE GOT!!
OKAY...
RUN LIKE A HORSE PULLING A CART!
OKAY, ATSU!
DASH
HUH?
MACHARU ?
WHERE'RE YOU GOING?
WHAT'S GOING ON?
ONE MEMBER IS LEAVING THE STUDIO...!

Is he going to the bathroom or something?
UMM... WHAT JUST HAPPENED HERE?
WHERE DID HE GO?
PROBABLY...
...TO GO SOLVE THE MOST IMPORTANT QUESTION.
HUH?
WHETHER OR NOT HE CAN SOLVE IT, THOUGH...
I SEE ...?
I COULDN'T HAVE PLANNED THAT BETTER WITH THE CAMERA.
WHAT'RE WE GONNA DO? NOW WE'RE DOWN TO FOUR!!
Ha.

YOU LOOK LIKE YOU'RE WELL.
Here it is.
I HEARD YOU TRANS-FERRED SCHOOLS.
IT SEEMS THAT I'VE CAUSED YOU A LOT OF PAIN. I FEEL BAD ABOUT THAT.
BUT...
THAT'S THE REALITY OF THE WORLD I LIVE IN.
DON'T WORRY.
I'M GOING TO CLIMB BACK UP AGAIN.

MUCH FARTHER THAN I DID BEFORE.
YOU DON'T NEED TO FEEL LIKE I'M KEEPING YOU BACK ANYMORE.
IT'S...
IT'S LIKE A MONKEY MOUN-TAIN...
SO WHAT CAN YOU SEE WHEN YOU'RE UP THERE?

DING
..DONG
BEEP
WHO IS IT?

OPEN
HUFF
MACHARU ?
HUFF
I...
...DON'T UNDER-STAND...
...HOW TO HELP YOU.
I HAVE NO IDEA...
...THE KINDS OF PROBLEMS THAT YOU MIGHT HAVE.

BUT...
I DO KNOW...
...I HATE IT WHEN YOU CRY AND I DON'T KNOW ABOUT IT.

...I CAN'T LEAVE YOU ALONE.
SO...
THAT MAKES YOUR PROBLEM ...
...MY PROBLEM.
THAT'S WHY...

HARUNA?
SHA
IS HE A FRIEND OF YOURS?

!!
YOUR DAD?
WHAT?
NO.
HE'S MY BOY-FRIEND.
OH?
I HAVE SOMEWHERE I NEED TO BE, DAD.
HUH?
WHERE?

WHAT?
LET'S GO, MACHARU.
MONKEYS ...?
IT FEELS LIKE I'M ON A MONKEY MOUNTAIN EVERYWHERE I GO.
BOW
SORRY FOR THE DISTURBANCE.
THAT'S WHAT IT SEEMS LIKE TO ME.
CLO
SE
BOY-FRIEND ?
EH...?
That guy ?!
WHERE THAT RIDICULOUS TROOP OF MONKEYS IS...

I WANT YOU TO BE BY MY SIDE LAUGHING.
BUT WHETHER I'M LOOKING UP OR LOOKING DOWN...
...IT DOESN'T MATTER WHERE WE ARE.
IT TURNS OUT...
"I HATE IT WHEN YOU CRY AND I DON'T KNOW ABOUT IT."

MAX
BEEP
BEEP
BEEP
BEEP
BEEP
THE METER'S UP! QUICK! ANSWER!
BING
REEF CRAB!
WE CAN'T EVEN SEE THE HEARTS...
...OF THE PEOPLE RIGHT NEXT TO US.

KITAYAMA HIGH SCHOOL HAS SOMEHOW MANAGED TO CLEAR THE RUNNING QUIZ AND IS WORKING THEIR WAY THROUGH THE STATIONARY BIKE QUIZ ROUND WITH TWO PEOPLE MISSING!
PANT
PANT
THAT IS CORRECT!
NICE!
AND IT LOOKS LIKE THEY'RE REACHING THEIR LIMIT!
Not possible.
...
WHEEZE
PANT
PANT
WHEEZE
WHEEZE
I NEED A BREAK...
SOMEONE...
BAM
SORRY TO KEEP YOU WAITING!
HEY, GUYS!

WOW..
WHAT'S THIS? KITAYAMA HIGH SCHOOL JUST REGAINED THE MISSING MEMBERS OF THEIR OVER-STRETCHED TEAM!
HUFF
HUFF
MACHARU!
HARUNA!
TAKE THE PRIZE!
#1
NOW FOR THE NEXT QUESTION ...
HOW'S THAT SUPPOSED TO HELP US?!
BUT THE RETURNING MEMBERS LOOK PRETTY TIRED AS WELL!
SO YOU HAVE NO INTENTION OF SWITCHING WITH ME...
ATSU! YOU'RE DOING GOOD!
GRRR..
HUFF COUGH
I forgot I'm just getting better...
COUGH
we pretty much sprinted here...
PANT PANT

AND SO...
WE...
...PUT UP A GOOD FIGHT TO THE END DESPITE OUR FATIGUE...
SCHOOL
*This picture is a conceptual image.
315
318
M HIGH SCHOOL QUIZ CLUB
286
KITAYAMA HIGH SCHOOL CLASS 1-2
221
HERE ARE THE RESULTS!

CLA
CLA
CLA
Congratulations.
OH... OUR TEN THOUSAND DOLLARS...
100
BUT WAIT! THERE'S MORE...
TO SHOW OUR APPRECIATION TO THE STUDENTS FROM KITAYAMA HIGH SCHOOL WHO...
...ALTHOUGH FINISHED LAST, PROVIDED US WITH QUALITY ENTERTAIN-MENT... WE WOULD LIKE TO PRESENT THEM WITH THE FIGHTING SPIRIT AWARD.
...BUT UNFORTUNATELY FINISHED LAST...
I'm not surprised...
No waaaay!
DROP

CAN YOU DESCRIBE WHAT YOU'RE FEELING FOR THE CAMERAS?
RIGHT... WE ACTUALLY ONLY CARE ABOUT THE PRIZE MONEY.
What kind of thanks is that?
And what kind of acceptance is that?
Fighting Spirit Award
I'M NOT SURE IF THIS WAS ALL INTENTIONAL, BUT THANKS FOR MAKING GREAT TV.
I AM DEFINITELY NOT PARTICIPATING NEXT YEAR!
WE PROMISE TO WIN NEXT YEAR!!
YOU DIDN'T HAVE FUN AT ALL?
Huh?
YEAH, RIGHT!
LOOKED LIKE YOU WERE ENJOYING YOURSELF TOO, HARUNA!
OH YEAH. WE'LL HAVE TO HAVE THE PRINCIPAL WAIT UNTIL NEXT YEAR!
THAT'S TRUE, HUH.

0
ESSION!
I HAD FUN, BUT NOT BECAUSE OF THE QUIZ SHOW...
IT WAS BECAUSE I WAS WITH YOU.
I DON'T WANT ANY MISUNDER-STANDINGS ABOUT THAT...
... DUMMY.

WHOOOOO
IT'S A LOVE
10,000
OH...
...NO...

NO THANK YOU!
Aren't you missing the point of the show?
WOW.
Best Couple Award
HERE'S A BEST COUPLE AWARD FOR THE TWO OF YOU.
clap clap clap clap
Whoo hoo!
THAT'S WHAT THEY GAVE US FOR THE FIGHTING SPIRIT AWARD.
TRAVEL COUPONS
J TRAVEL
HEY...
COOL! THEY'RE TRAVEL COUPONS!

DID YOU GUYS GET ANY-THING FOR THE BEST COUPLE AWARD?
WHY DON'T YOU GIVE THAT TO THE PRINCIPAL?
LET'S GO TO THE HOT SPRINGS!!
YAY!
NO WAY! THAT'S AWESOME !!
Probably the program staff...
WHO GAVE YOU THOSE?
YES
YEP. SEE? YES/NO PILLOWS.
UMM... EXCUSE ME, YOU GUYS.
Are they from the paparazzi again?
YOU SEE...
MISS HARUNA AIZAWA...
WE WERE WATCHING THE RECORDING JUST NOW, AND...

Don't come after us again!
RUN FOR IT!!
HEY!
WAIT...!
MAKING A BIG DEAL OUT OF EVERYTHING...

WORLDS ARE TURNED UPSIDE DOWN BY SIMPLE WORDS...
FROM THE OUTSIDE, IT'S AN UNBELIEVABLY SMALL WORLD...
"BUT IT'S ROOMY TOO."
BUT...

IT'S MY VERY OWN LOVEABLE MONKEY MOUNTAIN...

Love...?
MAYBE...
...AND...
...MY BABY MONKEY.
They were actually acting scouts...
ESPECIALLY THAT AIZAWA GIRL AND THE GUY WITH THE PIERCED EARS...
THEY WERE ALL GOOD MATERIAL ...
I WANTED TO GET THEM TO COME WORK FOR US.
DARN. THEY GOT AWAY...

Monkey High!

SPECIAL EDITION

SPECIAL EDITION

SPECIAL EDITION

THAT'S WHAT ATSU SAID...

"YOU LOOK GOOD WITH SHORT HAIR."

BUT...

LONG STRAIGHT HAIR THAT JUST FALLS SO BEAUTIFULLY, OR THE SOFT WAVES OF CURLY HAIR...

I'M ACTUALLY A LITTLE ENVIOUS, TO TELL YOU THE TRUTH...

MISATO! YOU CUT YOUR HAIR AGAIN!
MUSIC ROOM 2
YEAH, JUST A LITTLE.
YOU'RE RIGHT. I CAN SEE YOUR EARS.
I still don't get why you cut it....
THE MONKEY'S JUST INCREASING HER MONKEYNESS.
HIURA...
WHAT?
I'M ONLY TELLING THE TRUTH.

WELL, WHATEVER. I NEED YOU TO MOVE.
...
DON'T WORRY ABOUT WHAT HE SAYS, MISATO. YOU'RE ADORABLE.
Although I'm next to Misato, anyone looks like a giant...
HE'S SO TALL...
HIURA'S SCARY...
BUT...
WHY IS IT THAT YOU DON'T WANT TO GROW YOUR HAIR OUT?
THAT'S WHY I SAID, "INCREASING."
IT'S NOT THAT DIFFERENT.
You're always a monkey.

This is Atsu.
This is my older brother.
ATSU'S MY BROTHER'S FRIEND AND HE'S A FIRST YEAR IN HIGH SCHOOL.
HIS MOM RUNS THE LOCAL BEAUTY SALON.
YOU'RE NOT ALLOWED TO PERM OR DYE YOUR HAIR IN MIDDLE SCHOOL...
THERE'S A REASON I KEEP IT SHORT.
...SO IN ORDER TO GO TO THE BEAUTY SALON A LOT, THE ONLY CHOICE I'M LEFT WITH IS TO CUT MY HAIR FREQUENTLY.
ATSU IS AT THE BEAUTY SALON...
"YOU LOOK GOOD WITH SHORT HAIR."
AND THAT'S THE SAME ATSU WHO SAID...

"YOU LOOK CUTE. IT LOOKS GOOD ON YOU."

THAT'S WHEN I DECIDED TO GO GET IT CUT EVERY 20 DAYS.
I DON'T CARE IF I GO ONCE EVERY TWO WEEKS!

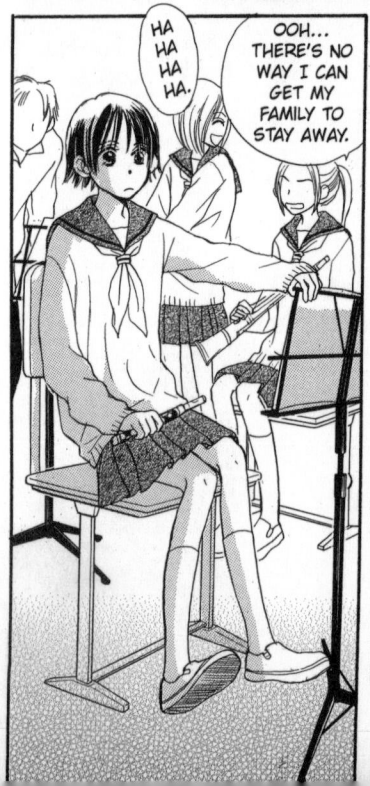
OOH... THERE'S NO WAY I CAN GET MY FAMILY TO STAY AWAY.
HA HA HA HA.

WOW--
IT'S A GOOD OPPORTUNITY TO HAVE YOUR FAMILY COME SEE YOU PERFORM.

I'VE GOT AN ANNOUNCEMENT TO MAKE BEFORE YOU BREAK OFF AND PRACTICE WITH YOUR SECTION.
WE'LL BE PERFORMING AT THE JOINT RECITAL AT THE TOWN HALL.

WE DON'T LOOK THAT MUCH ALIKE!!
NO. THEY ACTUALLY LOOK COMICALLY ALIKE...
WHY DON'T YOU HAVE YOUR BROTHER COME THEN?
IS MISATO'S BROTHER CUTE?
Huh?
WHAT ?
MY FAMILY HAS A BUSINESS, SO...
Probably not.
WHAT ABOUT YOU, MISATO?
THAT'S TOO BAD.
BUT...
HEY...
WHAT ...!
OH, C'MON. IT'S NOT LIKE YOU HAVE TO SHARE HIM...
YOU WANT TO SEE...?
PLEASE INVITE HIM!!
WHAT?! I WANNA SEE!
WH...
WHAT?
OH NOTHING... JUST...
...
I CAN ASK ATSU TO COME AS WELL.
THAT'S RIGHT, HUH.

IF YOU'RE PLANNING ON INVITING SOMEONE, YOU'D BETTER START PRACTICING.
CAUSE YOU'RE PRETTY BAD...
SHOCK
MISATO! YOU'RE LEAVING ALREADY?
IT'S ONLY JUST PAST SEVEN!
I'VE GOT SOMETHING I NEED TO TAKE CARE OF.
See you later!

I CAN'T PRACTICE AT HOME...
This is good.
I CAN FEEL IT VIBRATE.
OH...
PHOOO
AND THEN...
...I'M GOING TO HAVE ATSU COME SEE ME.
I'VE DECIDED.
I'M DEFINITELY GOING TO GET BETTER BEFORE THE RECITAL.

YOUR F IS OFF.
Oh, shoot...

I HEARD HIURA WAS IN A MARCHING BAND WHEN HE WAS IN GRADE SCHOOL.
FEE LA LEE LA FEE--
FEEE--
ARGH!!
I'M PARTICULARLY BAD...?
THAT'S BECAUSE ...
I FEEL LIKE HE PICKS ON ME IN PARTICULAR...
OR RATHER, THAT'S WHY HE ACTS SO CONDESCENDING!
THAT'S WHY HE WAS SO GOOD FROM THE BEGINNING.
He's pretty amazing.
That's the spirit, Misato!
I'M GONNA DO MY BEST!
I DON'T CARE!
BUT THE PICCOLO PART ON THE PIECE WE'RE DOING IS ESPECIALLY HARD!
DOOM

THE TIMING OF YOUR BREATHING'S OFF.
I'M PRACTICING EVERY DAY!
YOUR START TEMPO'S OFF.
WHAT'S THAT? A CALL FOR THE DEVIL?
THE RIVER FISH ARE GOING TO START COMPLAINING.
HIURA!!
You little...

THE BEGINNING OF THE SECOND MOVEMENT.
I HAVE A HARD TIME FIGURING IT OUT WHEN WE PRACTICE AS A BAND...
UM...
WHAT PART AM I DOING WRONG?
AND IT'S OFF FOR THE REST OF THE PIECE.
OR IF YOU DO, IT'S OFF.
YOU'VE GOT NO SOUND.
Urr... I officially hate you.
Emphasis on hard.
YOU JUST HAVE TO PRACTICE HARD, THAT'S ALL.
THANKS A LOT!
ALTHOUGH I DO ADMIT YOU'VE GOT COURAGE. TO WANT TO PERFORM WITH THAT KIND OF SKILL...
HA
THAT WAS A COMPLIMENT.

TA DAA
WOW! YOU'VE GOTTEN SO MUCH BETTER!
YEAH. IT SOUNDS GOOD.
THANKS!
JUST KEEP ON WORKING HARD! YOU'RE ON THE RIGHT TRACK!
Yay.

OOPS.
WHAT AM I DOING?
To Hiura, no less...
DON'T GET YOURSELF TOO PUMPED UP.
RECITAL?
YEAH.
I KNOW MOM AND DAD CAN'T GO...
AND EVERYONE ELSE'S FAMILIES ARE GOING...
I DON'T TRUST MASARU BEING THERE BY HIMSELF, SO...
WHAT'S THAT SUPPOSED TO MEAN?!
I SEE.
BREAK

SO BASICALLY, I'LL BE YOUR DAD...
...AND MACHARU CAN BE YOUR MOM, RIGHT?
YE...
YEAH...?
OH YEAH. YOU'RE IN THE BRASS BAND.
WHAT DO YOU PLAY?
SOMETHING LIKE THE GREAT DEMON KING, RIGHT?
IT'S CALLED A PICCOLO.
THIS IS TINY!
IT LOOKS LIKE A TOY!
NUH-UH! IT'S IN THE FLUTE FAMILY, AND IT SOUNDS REALLY PRETTY!
REALLY.
THEN...
...I'M LOOKING FORWARD TO YOUR PERFOR-MANCE.

I'LL BE THERE FOR SURE.
ATSU'S ALWAYS JOKING AROUND...
...BUT SOMETIMES HE SHOWS THE NICEST SMILE.
I'M GOING TO TRY TO "WOW" HIM...
Masaru said so too...
I THINK THAT'S WHAT MAKES HIM SUCH A PLAYER.
...AND MAKE HIM SEE I'M NOT A CHILD ANYMORE.
BUT I DON'T THINK HE HAS ONE NOW.
HE'S HAD AT LEAST THREE GIRLFRIENDS...
...THAT I KNOW OF.
Because he's always over.

HEY, GUYS! WE NEED TO GET READY.
GAH! THESE GUYS ARE GOOD.
WHAT ABOUT YOU, MISATO?
NOOOO! MY FAMILY'S IN THE SECOND ROW.
That sucks...
HA HA HA.
OH!
THEY'RE OVER THERE...
REALLY? WHICH ONE?

WAVE WAVE
HEY!
I KNOW WHICH ONE'S YOUR BROTHER!
HA HA HA. YOU GUYS REALLY DO LOOK ALIKE!
I TOLD YOU!
THEY NOTICED!
HEY!!
WHO'S THAT REALLY HOT GUY NEXT TO YOUR BROTHER?!
EEEEE...
DO YOU KNOW HIM, MISATO?
HE'S MY BROTHER'S FRIEND...
...ATSU.

And he came to see you?
HEH HEH.
I'm jealous!
HE'S SO HOT!
NO WAY!
YOU'RE ON A NICKNAME BASIS WITH HIM?
ATS ?!
WELL, HE LIVES CLOSE BY AND I'VE KNOWN HIM FOR A LONG TIME...
CALM DOWN A LITTLE BEFORE THE PERFORMANCE, WOULD YOU?
WHAT-EVER.
IT'S NONE OF YOUR BUSINESS, HIURA.

Jerk.
IF I MESS UP...?
MESS UP?
YOU'RE WRONG.
IT IS MY BUSINESS IF ONE OF YOU MESSES UP.

IF I MESS UP...
...ATSU'LL BE WATCHING...
IF I MESS UP...
NO...

HALL
THAT TOTALLY SUCKED.
CAN YOU BELIEVE SHE ACTUALLY DROPPED HER INSTRUMENT?
WHAT...?

WAIT A SEC...
MISATO... MY PARENTS CAME IN A CAR. YOU WANT A LIFT?
See you later.
B'bye!
I'LL BE FINE, REALLY. THANKS THOUGH.
ARE YOU SURE? IT LOOKS LIKE IT MIGHT RAIN...
HUH...? OH, THAT'S OKAY. I'LL BE FINE.
plip
plip
plip
SHAAA
ATSUYUKI!
WILL YOU PUT THE UMBRELLA STAND OUTSIDE?
SURE THING.
Hair KIDO

YOU LOOK TIRED.
I'LL LEND YOU A TOWEL AND AN UMBRELLA.
COME IN FOR A SEC.
HEY, THERE.
HOLD UP.
ATSU...

YEAH.
I GRABBED HER IN FRONT OF THE SALON.
YEAH. I'LL BRING HER HOME IN A BIT.
HEY, MACHAKO.
I'LL DRY YOUR HAIR FOR YOU. COME OVER HERE.
I'LL BE FINE...
IT'S SO SHORT, IT'LL DRY REALLY QUICK ANYWAY.
BUT IF YOU LET IT DRY LIKE THAT...
...YOU'LL LOOK EVEN MORE LIKE YOUR BROTHER...
Probably.
...
I DON'T CARE!
Whatever.
DON'T BE STUPID. YOU KNOW...

...I CAN'T LET A GIRL OUT OF THIS PLACE LOOKING LIKE THAT.
SEE...
...
MISATO?

...TO KEEP IT IN...
I TRIED SO HARD...
TUSSLE
TUSSLE

THIS SUCKS ...
I'M LIKE A KID...
HIURA...
...
Sakura Pens
Participation Award
YOU FORGOT THIS.
BUT HIS TIMING IS DEAD ON WHEN IT COMES TO STUFF LIKE THIS.
HE REALLY IS A WOMANIZER...

YOU BETTER NOT QUIT.
I...
I WON'T ...
OKAY THEN...
SEE YA.

SPLASH!
IS HE AN OLDER STUDENT IN THE BAND?
NO.
HE'S IN MY CLASS.
WHAT? HE'S IN 7TH GRADE?!
WOW! HE LOOKS SO OLD!!
I totally thought he was the captain or something.
...
AH... HE'S IN YOUR CLASS, HUH?
AND WAITING FOR YOU IN THIS KIND OF RAIN?
YOU GO, GIRL!
IT'S NOT LIKE THAT!!
YOU DON'T HAVE TO BE EMBARRASSED.
Sorry to be the third wheel.
ATSU, YOU IDIOT...!!
I DON'T KNOW WHAT'S GOING ON...
I'M SUPPOSED TO LIKE ATSU...

"YOU BETTER NOT QUIT."
BUT...

MORNIN'.
GOOD MORNING.
THANKS FOR COMING YESTERDAY!
SEE YOU TONIGHT!
WOW. SHE'S OFF TO SCHOOL AGAIN EARLY TODAY.
She left already?
know.
SHE WAS IN SUCH A DAZE AFTER SHE CAME HOME YESTERDAY...
I THOUGHT SHE WAS DEPRESSED.
She looks fine now.

THE TROMBONE HAS SUCH A SOFT SOUND.
I'D NEVER REALLY LISTENED TO IT BEFORE.

ALTHOUGH... DROPPING THE INSTRUMENT WOULD MAKE ANYBODY STAND OUT.
...
The trombone's pretty low-key by comparison...
GOOD OR BAD, IT STANDS OUT.
THE PICCOLO HAS THE HIGHEST SOUND OF THE ENTIRE BAND, SO...
...REALLY LIKED IT.
BUT THEN I STARTED PLAYING AND...
I EVEN THOUGHT, "THIS IS WAY BETTER!"
BUT THERE WERE SO MANY PEOPLE WHO WANTED TO...
I ENDED UP WITH THE PICCOLO.
... I... ACTUALLY WANTED TO PLAY THE FLUTE.

THE PICCOLO SUITS YOU.
IT'S SMALL AND...
...IT STANDS OUT.
HUH?
YOU JUST STARTED THOUGH.
...TO IMPROVE.
IT'S TAKING SO LONG...
BUT...

IT'S A GOOD FIT.
WHAT?
"IT'S A GOOD LOOK."
"YOUR SHORT HAIR...

IT'S ONLY JUST BEGUN...
THOSE WORDS ARE SPECIAL!
HUH?
WHY DO YOU HAVE TO SAY THAT?!
WHAT ARE YOU TALKING ABOUT?
MY HEART JUST SKIPPED A BEAT, THANKS TO YOU.
JEEZ ...
CLUB ACTIVITIES... FALLING IN LOVE...
EVEN IF IT'S ONE-SIDED...
THE PAIN AND THE POTENTIAL SWEETNESS... THE TRUE THRILL OF LIFE...
IT ALL LIES AHEAD.
MONKEY HIGH! SPECIAL EDITION *THE END*

★POSTSCRIPT★

THANK YOU FOR READING SHOUKO AKIRA'S MANGA.

I AM SO THANKFUL TO BE ABLE TO PUBLISH THIS SECOND VOLUME.

I'D LIKE TO USE THE REMAINING PAGES TO LOOK BACK ON EACH OF THE STORIES.

Plus it's only 40 pages! This is going to be a breeze!

YES!!

THE FOURTH STORY (ABOUT THE FIRST DATE)

THIS TIME, IT'S A DATE! THERE'S ONLY TWO OF THEM!

THE SCHOOL SCENES WERE HARD TO DRAW WITH SO MANY STUDENTS, BUT...

HOW WRONG I WAS...

MY LITTLE SISTER'S BITTER OUTBURST
WHAT IS MACHARU DOING LAYERING UP ANYWAY?
NOW THAT WE'RE ON THE SUBJECT, THE SCREEN-TONE ON MACHARU'S CLOTHES IS A REAL PAIN TOO.
mumble
mumble
It was actually the biggest pain for my assistant, who was forced to draw all the backgrounds...
AN AMUSEMENT PARK IS THE BIGGEST PAIN OF ALL...

Although out of any mascot I've seen at amuse-ment parks, this may be the least cute of them all...
ATSU HAD THE SWEETEST DEAL...

THE FIFTH STORY
(ABOUT THE QUIZ SHOW)
BUT I DON'T WANT TO MESS WITH THE EXISTING TIMELINE, SO IT'LL BE ABOUT A MONTH AFTER THAT FIRST DATE...
It's the October issue... Is that okay?
IT HAS TO BE EASY TO UN-DERSTAND FOR PEOPLE WHO HAVEN'T BEEN FOLLOWING THE STORY, AND IT HAS TO HAVE A SELF-CONTAINED PLOT.
THIS REALLY TURNED MY WORLD UPSIDE DOWN...
MONKEY HIGH! WAS FEATURED IN A SPECIAL EDITION OF BETSUCOMI, BUT WITH THIS ONE, I WAS GIVEN 100 PAGES IN THE ACTUAL BETSUCOMI MAGAZINE.
I HAD 100 PAGES, SO I WANTED IT TO BE A BIG EVENT.
But there aren't that many school events that take place over the course of a month... An all-school marathon?

I FEEL LIKE THIS WAS CLOSER TO MY NORMAL ONE-SHOT STORIES THAN THE *MONKEY HIGH!* FORMULA...

THE SPECIAL EDITION (MACHAKO'S STORY)

THE MIDDLE SCHOOL DIARIES

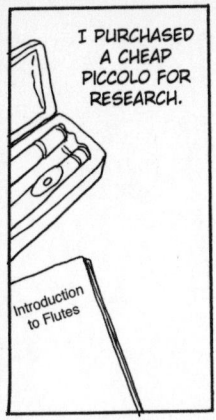

I ENVY PEOPLE WHO ARE MUSICALLY TALENTED.

AS YOU CAN SEE, I DON'T HAVE ANY MUSICAL GENES IN MY BODY...BUT I DO HAVE SOME FRIENDS IN A WIND INSTRUMENT BAND, SO I OFTEN WENT TO SEE THEM PERFORM.

ARE YOU SERIOUS?!

IN ALL HONESTY, I WAS A LITTLE SHOCKED. WHEN I STARTED THIS SERIES, I WONDERED IF IT WAS OKAY TO HAVE THE HERO BE SOMEONE WHO WAS UNPOPULAR WITH GIRLS...

AFTER I PUBLISHED VOLUME ONE, I GOT LETTERS FROM READERS SAYING THEY LIKED MACHARU OR THAT THE PERSON THEY HAVE A CRUSH ON IS A LOT LIKE MACHARU.

I'D LIKE TO THANK EVERYONE WHO IS ALWAYS HELPING ME—MY EDITOR, DESIGNERS, FRIENDS, ACQUAINTANCES AND ALL MY READERS! THANK YOU SO VERY MUCH. I ASK FOR YOUR CONTINUED SUPPORT, AND I'LL DO MY BEST TO CREATE A FUN STORY FOR YOUR ENJOYMENT.

DECEMBER 2005
SHOUKO AKIRA

Slightly confused by all the monkeying around? Here are some notes to help you out!

Page 2: **Masaru**
Even though everyone refers to him by his nickname, Macharu's real name is "Masaru," which means "superior" in Japanese. Interestingly enough, *saru* by itself means "monkey."

Page 62, panel 2: **The Diet**
Japan's parliament is called the Diet; it consists of the House of Representatives and the House of Councillors. In addition to passing laws, the Diet is responsible for selecting the Prime Minister.

Page 72, panel 4: **Arashi, w-inds, and KAT-TUN**
All Japanese boy bands. Arashi has five members, w-inds has three and KAT-TUN has six.

Page 100, panel 4: **Nikko**
One of the things the Tosho-gu shrine in Nikko is famous for is its carving of the three wise monkeys who embody the principle "see no evil, hear no evil, speak no evil."

Page 160, panel 3: **The Great Demon King**
A reference to the fictional character Piccolo in the manga series *Dragon Ball Z*.

Page 185, panel 4: ***Betsucomi***
A monthly Japanese *shojo* manga (girls' comics) magazine published by Shogakukan.

My jeans have become noticeably tighter... And they're the pair that I wear all the time... I've gotta do something about this...

—Shouko Akira

Shouko Akira was born on September 10th and grew up in Kyoto. She currently lives in Tokyo and loves soccer, cycling, and Yoshimoto Shin Kigeki (a comedy stage show based out of Osaka). Most of her works revolve around school life and love, including *Times Two*, a collection of five romantic short stories.

MONKEY HIGH!
VOL. 2
The Shojo Beat Manga Edition

STORY AND ART BY
SHOUKO AKIRA

Translation & Adaptation/Mai Ihara
Touch-up Art & Lettering/John Hunt
Design/Hidemi Dunn
Editor/Amy Yu

Editor in Chief, Books/Alvin Lu
Editor in Chief, Magazines/Marc Weidenbaum
VP of Publishing Licensing/Rika Inouye
VP of Sales/Gonzalo Ferreyra
Sr. VP of Marketing/Liza Coppola
Publisher/Hyoe Narita

© 2006 Shouko AKIRA/Shogakukan Inc.
First published by Shogakukan Inc. in Japan as "Saruyama!"
All rights reserved.
The stories, characters and incidents mentioned in this publication are entirely fictional.

No portion of this book may be reproduced or transmitted in any form or by any means without written permission from the copyright holders.

Printed in Canada

Published by VIZ Media, LLC
P.O. Box 77010
San Francisco, CA 94107

Shojo Beat Manga Edition
10 9 8 7 6 5 4 3 2 1
First printing, June 2008

www.viz.com

store.viz.com

PUNCH!™

By Rie Takada

She hails from a family of kickboxing champions, but Elle's a lover, not a fighter, and she's sick and tired of the boys at her grandfather's gym chasing away all of her potential suitors! When a cute and scrappy street brawler captures her attention, she decides he's worth fighting for!

Final Volume!

Only $8.99 each

Shojo Beat™
MANGA from the HEART

On sale at:
www.shojobeat.com
Also available at your local bookstore and comic store.

Punch! © 2005 Rie TAKADA/Shogakukan Inc.
Covers subject to change.

viz media™
www.viz.com

I•O•N

By Arina Tanemura,
creator of *Full Moon* and *The Gentlemen's Alliance †*

Ion Tsuburagi is a normal junior high girl with normal junior high problems. But when a mysterious substance grants her telekinetic powers, she finds herself struggling to keep everything together! Are her new abilities a blessing...or a curse?

Find out in *I•O•N*—manga on sale now!

On sale at www.shojobeat.com
Also available at your local bookstore and comic store.

I•O•N © 1997 by Arina Tanemura/SHUEISHA Inc.

www.viz.com

The gripping story – in manga format

Get the complete *Be With You* collection—buy the manga and fiction today!

Ima Ainiyukimasu © Sai KAWASHIMA, Takuji ICHIKAWA, Yoko IINO/Shogakukan Inc.
Ima Ainiyukimasu © Takuji ICHIKAWA/Shogakukan Inc.

ratings.viz.com

www.viz.com

Be With You

Is it possible to experience first love
for a second time?

The answer, as *Be With You* proves, is yes—
a million times yes

The **hit novel** that inspired the manga series

SB FICTION

Shojo Beat
MANGA from the HEART

On sale at:
www.shojobeat.com
Also available at your local bookstore and comic store.

Beauty Pop

By Kiyoko Arai

Although a truly gifted hairstylist, Kiri Koshiba has no interest in using her talent to pursue fame and fortune, unlike the three popular boys in the "Scissors Project" at school. They give showy makeovers to handpicked girls, determined to become the best makeover team in Japan. As much as Kiri tries to shy away from the Scissors Project spotlight, she finds herself responding to beauty's call...

Shojo Beat™
MANGA from the HEART

Only $8.99

On sale at:
www.shojobeat.com
Also available at your local bookstore and comic store.

Beauty Pop © 2004 Kiyoko ARAI/Shogakukan Inc.
Covers subject to change.

www.viz.com

Shojo Beat
S•A
Special A
by Maki Minami
Manga series on sale now
Only $8.99
Shojo Beat Manga
S•A
Maki Minami
Her whole life, Hikari Hanazono has been consumed with the desire to win against her school rival, Kei Takishima—at anything. He always comes out on top no matter what he does, and Hikari is determined to do whatever it takes to beat him!
Shojo Beat
MANGA from the HEART
On sale at:
www.shojobeat.com
Also available at your local bookstore and comic store.
S • A-Special A© Maki Minami 2003/HAKUSENSHA, Inc.
RATED T FOR TEEN
ratings.viz.com
viz media
www.viz.com

Tell us what you think about Shojo Beat Manga!
Our survey is now available online. Go to:
shojobeat.com/mangasurvey
Help us make our product offerings better!
viz media
Shojo Beat
THE REAL DRAMA BEGINS IN...
FULL MOON WO SAGASHITE © 2001 by Arina Tanemura/SHUEISHA Inc.
Fushigi Yûgi: Genbu Kaiden © 2004 Yuu WATASE/Shogakukan Inc.
Ouran Koko Host Club © Bisco Hatori 2002/HAKUSENSHA, Inc.

Shojo Beat™

MANGA from the HEART

The Shojo Manga Authority

The most ADDICTIVE shojo manga stories from Japan PLUS unique editorial coverage on the arts, music, culture, fashion, and much more!

12 GIANT issues for ONLY $34.99*

That's 51% OFF the cover price!

Subscribe NOW and become a member of the Sub Club!

- SAVE 51% OFF the cover price
- ALWAYS get every issue
- ACCESS exclusive areas of www.shojobeat.com
- FREE members-only gifts several times a year

Strictly VIP!

3 EASY WAYS TO SUBSCRIBE!

1) Send in the subscription order form from this book OR
2) Log on to: www.shojobeat.com OR
3) Call 1-800-541-7876

Canada price for 12 issues: $46.99 USD, including GST, HST and QST. US/CAN orders only. Allow 6-8 weeks for delivery. Must be 16 or older to redeem offer. By redeeming this offer I represent that I am 16 or older.
Vampire Knight © Matsuri Hino 2004/HAKUSENSHA, Inc. Nana Kitade © Sony Music Entertainment (Japan), Inc.
SHOJO EVE ★ EVE'S APPLEWORK 24 HOURS © 2007 by Arina Tanemura/SHUEISHA Inc.
CRIMSON HERO © 2002 by Mitsuba Takanashi/SHUEISHA Inc.

RATED T FOR OLDER TEEN ratings.viz.com

viz media
www.viz.com

Save OVER 50% off the cover price!

FREMONT PUBLIC LIBRARY
3 3090 00349 1836

Shojo Beat

MANGA from the HEART

The Shojo Manga Authority

This monthly magazine is injected with the most **ADDICTIVE** shojo manga stories from Japan. PLUS, unique editorial coverage on the arts, music, culture, fashion, and much more!

☑ **YES!** Please enter my one-year subscription (12 GIANT issues) to ***Shojo Beat*** at the LOW SUBSCRIPTION RATE of **$34.99!**

Over 300 pages per issue!

NAME

ADDRESS

CITY STATE ZIP

E-MAIL ADDRESS P7GNC1

☐ MY CHECK IS ENCLOSED (PAYABLE TO *Shojo Beat*) ☐ BILL ME LATER

CREDIT CARD: ☐ VISA ☐ MASTERCARD

ACCOUNT # EXP. DATE

SIGNATURE

CLIP AND MAIL TO

SHOJO BEAT
Subscriptions Service Dept.
P.O. Box 438
Mount Morris, IL 61054-0438

Canada price for 12 issues: $46.99 USD, including GST, HST and QST. US/CAN orders only. Allow 6-8 weeks for delivery. Must be 16 or older to redeem offer. By redeeming this offer I represent that I am 16 or older.

Vampire Knight © Matsuri Hino 2004/HAKUSENSHA, Inc. Nana Kitade © Sony Music Entertainment (Japan), Inc.
CRIMSON HERO © 2002 by Mitsuba Takanashi/SHUEISHA Inc.

RATED T FOR OLDER TEEN
ratings.viz.com

3-09